How to Play the Ocarina

A Beginner's Guide to Learning the Flute
Basics, Reading Music, and Playing Songs
(with 10+ Audio Guides)

By: Cynthia Riess

Table of Contents

Throughout this book there are musical examples and audio recordings to follow along with on your journey to learn how to play the ocarina.

Whenever you see the following outline:

1. C Major Scale

Please follow along with the recordings at the following website: https://bit.ly/3J9XeEq

Or use the QR Code Below:

Chapter 1

Introduction and Overview

Congratulations on taking the first step in your ocarina journey! It can seem difficult or challenging to start a new instrument, but with lots of time and practice, one can begin to build their skillset on any instrument.

The ocarina is an instrument that can be played by basically everyone, even someone lacking prior musical experience. The sound of the ocarina can vary from long, gentle, low tones to higher, fast sounds that can bring you lots of excitement and intrigue as you master the techniques required to play this instrument.

This guide will teach you everything you need to know when beginning the ocarina and the steps you will need to take afterward. By the end of this guide, you will have learned many key lessons that will help you grow in your ocarina and musical abilities.

What is an Ocarina?

The **ocarina** is a relatively uncommon instrument, as it is not typically played by people in the modern era. However, it may be well known to those who have played games such as *EarthBound Beginnings*, *The Legend of Zelda: Ocarina of Time*, or *The Legend of Zelda: Majora's Mask*, which feature the ocarina throughout as a gameplay mechanic. The instrument is also heavily featured in the soundtrack!

It is surprising that more people don't play this instrument, as the ocarina is a great instrument for beginners. Its incredible accessibility makes it perfect for all types of people; even while purchasing a higher-quality ocarina, you can still stay on a budget.

The ocarina can be made from a variety of materials, including plastic, wood, and ceramics. While ocarinas can be made from virtually any material, these will be the most common and the highest quality for playing.

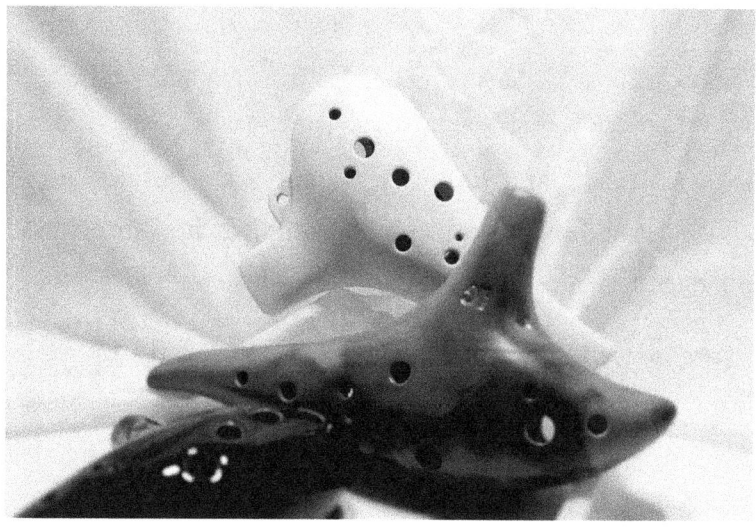

The ocarina is a **wind instrument**, and it is classified as a type of **vessel flute**. Specifically, a vessel flute is a type of flute in which the body works as a Helmholtz resonator. The end of the instrument is closed—thus why it is 'vessel'-shaped. This contrasts with the typical build of a flute (with an open end), creating a distinct difference between these instrument types. Any instrument in this family is known for producing sound by the player blowing air into the mouthpiece, like other wind instruments.

This instrument can exist in a variety of forms, and each may appear different from the last. However, an ocarina is best identified by having a smooth, roundish body and many open holes within the body, which are pressed down in a variety of ways to achieve your desired note. The number of **finger holes** can vary from four to twelve, along with a **mouthpiece** that stems out from the **body** of the instrument.

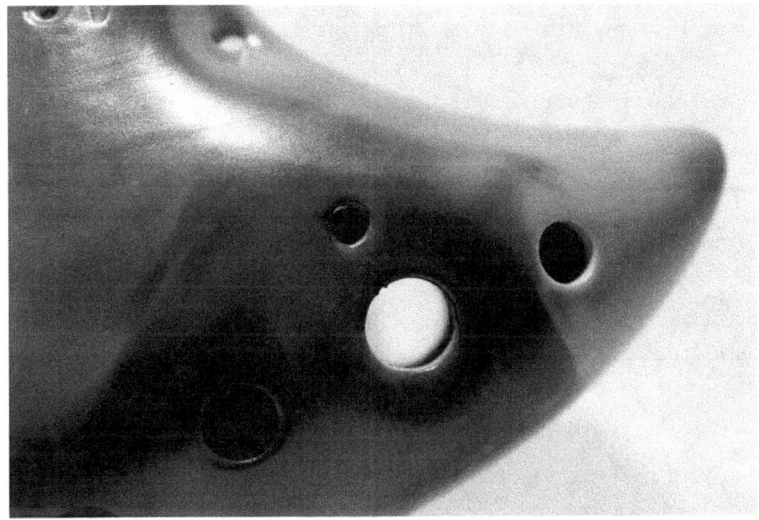

While there are many distinct types of ocarinas, and some people will play multiple variations, <u>**this guide will primarily focus on 12-hole ocarinas**</u>, as these are the most common type for players of all skill levels. However, this guide will still prove helpful to people with other ocarina types in terms of technique and playing recommendations.

The History of the Ocarina

The ocarina has been around for thousands of years, with some archaeologists stating that it has been around for as many as 12,000 years. The ocarina has existed across a variety of cultures and in many different forms, meaning that it also has an array of appearances and sounds.

Over time, the ocarina has only become more popular. Many iterations are even able to play chromatic scales! Such a feat would not have been possible with the previous versions of this instrument and without great innovation.

The early history of the ocarina is not well-known, but these instruments have been found in Mexico, Colombia, Egypt, Central Africa, India, China, Korea, and Japan, along with having deep roots in pre-Classic Mesoamerica. Because its history is both so wide-ranging and ancient, the invention of the instrument comes with speculation.

Historically, these instruments have been referred to as vessel flutes, which were often made from clay and resembled birds, animals, people, and cultural symbols varying on the originators of the given ocarina.

Around 7000 years ago in ancient China, there was an instrument called the Xun, which was an egg-shaped vessel flute. The Xun was made from either clay or ceramics, looking like the ocarina and proving to be a beautiful precursor to the modern instrument.

In Korea, the traditional ocarina is known as the hun, while the Japanese ocarina is called a tsuchibue.

Archaeological finds prove that both the Maya and Aztecs produced versions of the ocarina. In addition to this, the Aztecs brought the ocarina to Europe, along with traditional song and dance.

In 1964, English mathematician John Taylor developed a distinct fingering method to allow musicians to play a complete chromatic scale on the ocarina with only four finger holes. This only works on a select number of ocarina types, but it shows the development of this instrument over time. The playing of this instrument has become more streamlined due to increased knowledge. With this increase in knowledge, there is also more for you to learn!

So, when it comes to playing the ocarina, it is important to remember the vast history of this instrument and the cultural significance that it holds to a variety of people across the world. While this instrument may not be regularly played to this day, its existence in our contemporary era is a testament to the importance of art and culture throughout history. To get a good feel for this instrument, it can be helpful to research its historic sound and original instrumentation to get inspiration.

The elegant sound of this instrument has been loved by many cultures and continues to be loved to this day. Learning the ocarina isn't limited by your age or previous knowledge of music. Moreover, the ocarina's expressive potential allows the player to tell stories in a variety of manners, whether emotional and gushing or quick and peppy.

Whether you are a beginner or an experienced musician looking to pick up a new instrument, the ocarina promises you a new experience and journey that will musically enrich your life.

Ocarina Anatomy

When it comes to describing the ocarina, it can be broken down simply. There are no additional parts or screws necessary to assemble this instrument, which makes this a great instrument for those looking for simplicity.

The exact anatomy of your ocarina will depend on your instrument. Because of the diverse history of this instrument, there are also different types and forms that it may take. However, each ocarina will generally have the same parts, though they may appear in different places on the instrument.

The ocarina, at its most basic form, is made up of a body, a mouthpiece, and finger holes.

The **body** of the ocarina is going to be vessel-shaped. It could be made from porcelain, ceramic, wood, metal, or plastic, among other materials. The body is what you will hold when playing the ocarina. Based on the way your ocarina has been made, you may need to figure out the most comfortable way to hold your instrument. Keep in mind that holding the body of your ocarina should feel natural and cause little to no strain on your hands and fingers.

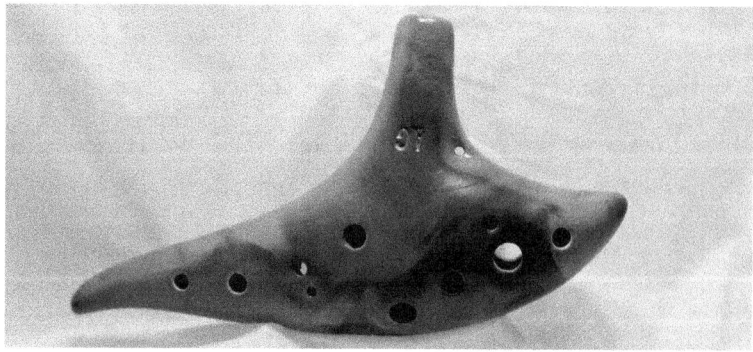

Next, the **mouthpiece** stems from the body of the ocarina. It will be quite easy to recognize, as it sticks out from the smooth-bodied instrument. To play the ocarina, one must blow air into the mouthpiece. It is not difficult to make a sound on this instrument, as the **embouchure**—the positioning of your face, lips, and tongue as you blow air into your instrument—is relatively natural. This guide will later cover more on how to make a sound on your ocarina.

Finally, there are the **finger holes**. These are the circular gaps on the body of your ocarina, which can quite easily be covered by one's finger. Some players may also refer to these as **tone holes**. These can be broken down into subcategories based on which finger holes one is referring to.

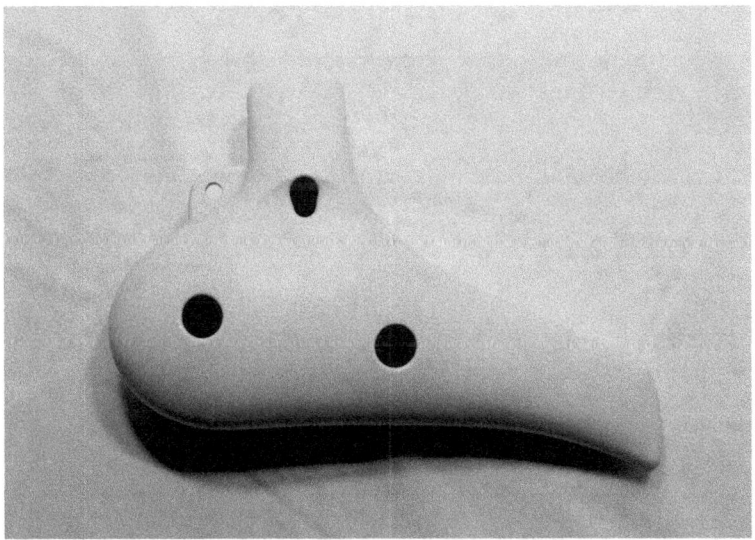

Notably, the two holes found on the back of the ocarina are called **thumb holes,** while the minuscule gaps on the front side of your instrument are known as **sub holes**.

You may notice that there is a somewhat large opening on the back of your ocarina. In the center middle of your instrument, beneath the mouthpiece, there is a gap that appears different from the rest of your finger holes. This is because this is the **voicing** or **whistle**. This should not be covered when you play, as it is necessary to produce your instrument's sound.

Consider a typical 12-hole ocarina: when resting your hands on the instrument, you will put your right hand on top of the ocarina's body while your left will support the body from beneath. Your thumbs should be on the backside of the instrument, while your eight other fingers should be on the front. From here, you will be easily able to move and hit your desired notes by adjusting your fingers' positioning.

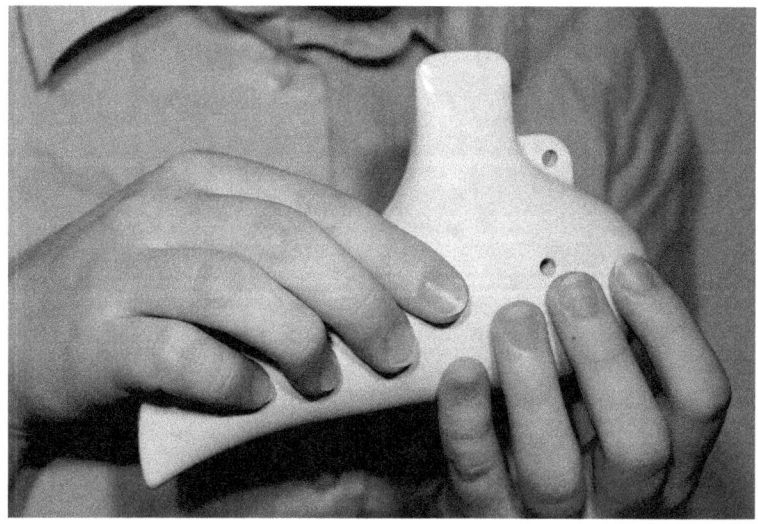

Chapter 2

Selecting and Buying the Correct Instrument

Types and Features of the Ocarina

As discussed previously, there are a variety of ocarina types. This instrument is incredibly diverse, and each one can be built differently. While two instruments may look incredibly distinct, they can still produce a similar sound. This is a unique feature of the ocarina, and it makes it even more difficult to select the perfect instrument for your needs!

When it comes to making the final decision about which ocarina you would like to purchase, you should keep in mind your musical intentions, how serious do you envision your ocarina playing to be?

If you are unsure of how serious your playing may become, it is a good idea to set up a lower budget for a beginner instrument, knowing that you can always invest in a higher-quality instrument further down the line. The best ocarinas are going to be a little pricier, so you are going to want to make sure this hobby is something you are willing to financially invest in before spending that sort of money. However, a cheap beginner instrument—one that you can use to get a feel for the ocarina—can be incredibly helpful when you are deciding whether you want to invest additional money into this new hobby.

It is recommended that beginners—especially those looking to save money—purchase a cheaper, mass-produced instrument. You should be sure to look for ones with complimentary reviews and, notably, ones that produce a high-quality, in-tune sound. However, if you would like to prioritize looks or aesthetics when it comes to buying a beginner instrument, this is not an issue, as this stage of learning is mostly for getting a feel for the ocarina in your hands.

Plastic ocarinas will most likely be the cheapest ones available for purchase online, and these are perfect for what you need.

When purchasing an ocarina online, you should be sure to read the reviews on the instrument, both from the sites that you are planning on purchasing your ocarina through and beyond. If you can't find anyone talking about your desired instrument or its brand online, you should likely reconsider purchasing that ocarina. Since you are a beginner, it is a good idea to set yourself up for success in every possible aspect and get a positively-reviewed instrument.

There are many places you can easily purchase an ocarina from. Whether you go through a big supplier, music store, or small ocarina business, you are likely to get a good instrument.

Keep in mind that this guide caters to the most common ocarina type, which is a **12-hole Alto C ocarina**. This is also the most common ocarina type, so it is a good place for beginners to start as they explore the range of this instrument. If you choose to learn from a different type of ocarina, this guide will still apply to you, though it may require some musical translation.

Soprano, Alto, or Bass Ocarina?

There are a variety of ocarina types, based often on the number of finger holes and the octave range. This section will cover the differences in octave range, which can be helpful when initially determining which instrument you would like to purchase.

The ocarina tends to be higher pitched when compared to other woodwind instruments, and this is for a variety of reasons. Firstly, there is no musical standardization for the ocarina, and secondly, this is an instrument that also sounds phenomenal at higher pitches when compared to other woodwinds, which may have a harder time difficulty maintaining such quality sound.

Previously, this guide referred to an **alto ocarina**. This describes an ocarina with a pitch range anywhere between A4 to F6, with the letters (in this example, 'A' or 'F') detailing the pitch of the note and the following number describing the octave that pitch occurs in.

Because there is no standard for making an ocarina, this is only the typical range. Sometimes, ocarinas made in Korea or France may differ and have slightly different ranges.

While there is the alto ocarina, there are also ocarinas that have higher and lower pitch ranges. The **soprano ocarina** is going to have a pitch range of usually about 10-12 notes, starting at around F6 and going upwards.

Typically, the range beneath alto is referred to as tenor. But in the case of the ocarina, bass ocarinas are going to be in the tenor range, despite their name. The **bass ocarina** will usually have its highest note be around A4, with everything else descending in pitch frequency.

All three of these ocarina types have their benefits, unique sound quality, and differences in playing technique.

Again, the most common type for the beginner player is the alto ocarina. Since they are in the middle range of the musical staff, it will be easier for you to find sheet music that fits your instrument. It is a good mid-point between beautiful low notes and the singing high notes of the ocarina.

The soprano ocarina may be beneficial for those with smaller hands. This slightly smaller instrument is easy to handle and will require you to cover less space. It will be able to hit higher notes, as well, and highlight the amazing, airy qualities of the ocarina.

In contrast, the bass ocarina is going to be a little bit bigger, with the ability to hit far lower notes. This instrument will produce a deeper, more mellow sound.

Each person is going to have to make their own decision when it comes to the model they would like to purchase, as each one has its own benefits and drawbacks.

Unless you are profoundly serious about your future in ocarina playing, there will likely not be a need for you to purchase anything more than an alto ocarina, as this is a relatively common and standard instrument for an ocarina player to have.

Even if you do not plan to purchase any additional types of ocarinas, it is helpful to know the differences between them.

Choosing the Right One

Ultimately, selecting the 'right' ocarina is going to be a completely subjective choice. What you may desire from your instrument could be completely different from someone else, which is why this guide does not make specific reference to the 'best' ocarina out there (spoiler: the 'best' ocarina does not exist!).

So long as you can get your hands on an instrument that you are satisfied with, then you are ready to begin working with this instrument and diving into the beautiful world of the ocarina.

Chapter 3

Knowing Your Instrument

Understanding the Basics

When it comes to the very basics, the ocarina is a self-explanatory instrument. The grip is incredibly natural to the human hand, and blowing air into the mouthpiece of the instrument will easily produce sound. There is not much of an embouchure required to make an initial noise on this instrument. Putting your lips around the mouthpiece—in combination with a given arrangement of your fingers covering the finger holes—will produce a note.

It is important to keep in mind, however, that learning how to play the ocarina is not about the basics but about mastering these basics. Over time, you will learn how to adjust the muscles in your face and the placement of your tongue in your mouth to create notes that are well-produced, clear, and of the correct pitch.

While initially playing around with the ocarina, it is a good idea to move your fingers over the finger holes. Try moving up and down the instrument; get used to the feeling of adjusting the ocarina in your hands.

Additionally, try picking your ocarina up and blowing into it. If you do not know what finger holes to cover, you will likely produce a sound that doesn't replicate an exact musical note, but that's okay: the ocarina is a playful instrument that calls for experimentation! Don't be scared to try messing around with the ocarina and seeing what sounds you can make and if there are any you recognize as more soothing to your ears (i.e., in tune).

When holding the ocarina, make sure your posture is good. You will want to have both your feet resting flat on the floor and your back straight. You don't need to be sitting to play the ocarina, but this will likely be more comfortable for extended periods of play. Be sure to set your shoulders back when drawing the ocarina up to your lips and not to slouch forward! You are going to produce your best and clearest notes when sitting up straight, as this makes it easier for your lungs to draw in deep breaths, which will, in turn, allow you to put more air into your instrument.

By blowing air into your instrument, you are creating resonant **sound waves** that will move through the vessel-shaped body of the ocarina and make noise.

The sounds that you make on your ocarina in the beginning may not be the best, but this is okay! Actually, it's more than okay! This is as expected! As you learn more about how to play the ocarina, you will get better at producing a quality sound. Practice and time are going to take you far with this instrument, just as it will with any other.

Caring For Your Ocarina

Luckily for you, the ocarina is an incredibly easy instrument to care for. Your ocarina will also likely be very sturdy. This means that dropping one (especially a plastic one) may not break your instrument. For obvious reasons (i.e., shattering your beloved ocarina), this method of handling is not encouraged. However, it is nice to know that dropping your ocarina will not cause the end of the world or a very pricy trip to the music store for repairs.

To protect your ocarina, however, you should store the instrument in a safe location whenever you are not actively playing it. Leaving your ocarina in a place where it could get picked up and/or thrown around by a pet, young child, or sibling could lead to the quality of your instrument getting worse over time, especially when it is being handled improperly. While your first ocarina will not be expensive when compared to the cost of other musical instruments, it is still possible to avoid additional costs by simply always keeping your ocarina in a safe location.

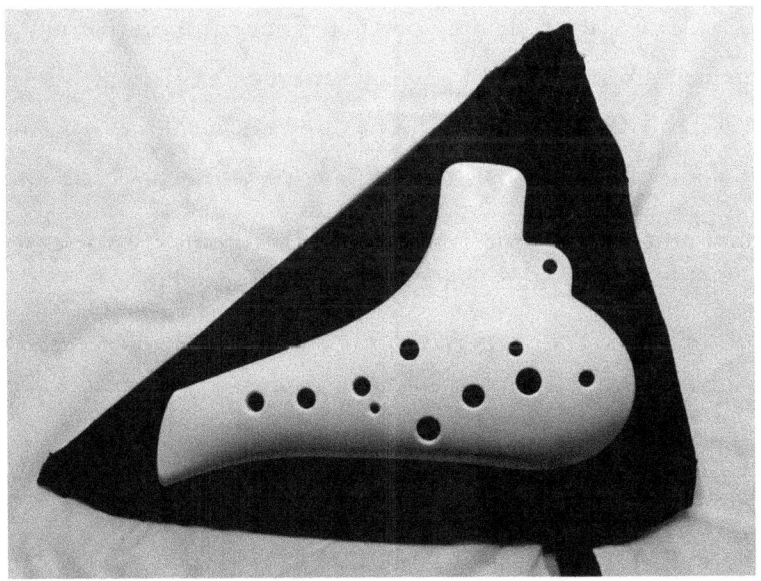

Ocarinas can be made from wood. If you have a wooden ocarina, it is important to store this type of ocarina in a place where it will not receive any water damage or residual damage from humidity. This means that leaving a wooden ocarina out in the open air of your home could gradually lead to the instrument's quality lessening. By keeping your ocarina in a case whenever you are not playing it, you ensure it will not get damaged over time. Looking after your instrument, even when you are not playing it, is one of the most important things a musician can do!

Unlike many other woodwind instruments, there is not a common way to clean out the ocarina. This is because there are simply so many types and materials out there that it is impossible to create one distinct method that is inclusive of all finishes, polishes, and natural materials.

The most common method for ocarina cleaning is going to involve the use of a polishing or microfiber cloth on the outside of the instrument (to remove any fingerprints), along with running a thin strip of paper through the mouthpiece of the instrument to clean out any debris or residual spit inside the body. If you are concerned about the cleanliness of your ocarina beyond this, you may be able to run a lint-free cloth lightly doused in water through the instrument. However, if you have a wooden instrument, this is not a recommended strategy.

Additionally, avoid the use of strong chemicals, which could also affect you when playing in the future, as your lips and fingers do come directly in contact with the mouthpiece and body of the instrument.

Accessorizing Your Ocarina

This instrument does not have many common accessories, if any. This is because any sort of accessory you come across is going to be purely aesthetic and rarely serves a musical function.

One common accessory that you may get upon receiving your first ocarina is a cord that you can weave through the hole to the side of the mouthpiece of your instrument so you can wear your ocarina as a necklace. People do this—especially if they are dressing up and using the ocarina as a prop—to keep the instrument around their neck so they may play whenever the desire strikes them. The ocarina, thankfully, is not heavy enough to cause strain on your arms, hands, or neck, with or without such a cord.

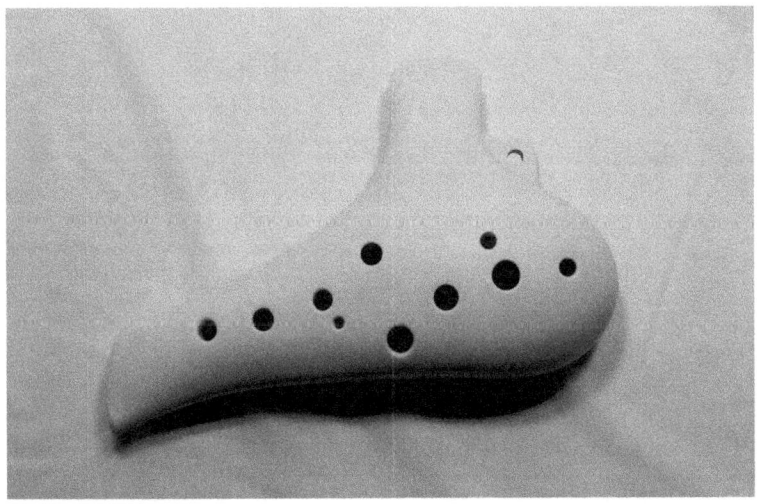

Another type of accessory that you may receive with your ocarina is a stand to keep your instrument on. If you receive one of these and feel a powerful desire to display your instrument, go for it! It is recommended, however, that you pick a safe location for your ocarina so you can avoid the instrument being broken. Placing your ocarina on a stand within a safe location such as a bookshelf may prove a beautiful way to spice up your room as well as keep your instrument in your line of sight, so you never forget to keep up with your playing!

Overall, the ocarina is not a difficult instrument to look after, and this makes it a great option for beginners or people looking for simplicity in their creative lives. The accessibility of this instrument opens the door to the brilliant world of music for many people. So, if you hear it calling to you, do not shy away from it!

Now that you have gotten familiar with your instrument, you are almost ready to play.

Chapter 4

How To Play the Ocarina

Topics Covered:

- How to produce a sound

- Keeping your fingers moving

- What it means to play "in tune"

- Playing melodies on the ocarina

You are ready to pick up your instrument (with the correct posture!) and play. Throughout this chapter, you will start to play the ocarina and learn the basics of this beautiful instrument.

Producing a Sound

There is not a lot required to make a sound on the ocarina. For an easy first note, try covering the holes of your ocarina, as shown in the picture below.

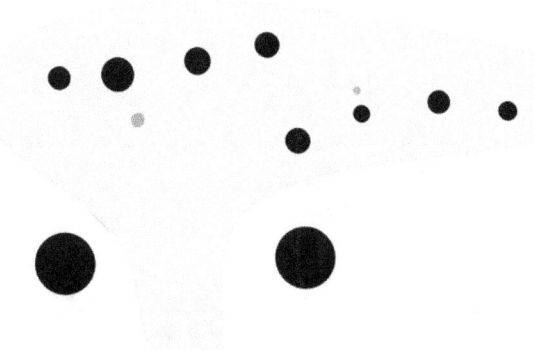

Essentially, cover every finger hole beside the sub-holes.

From there, lift the instrument to your lips and blow into the mouthpiece. Make sure your lips are around the mouthpiece and that there are not any noticeable gaps. From there, you will produce a note.

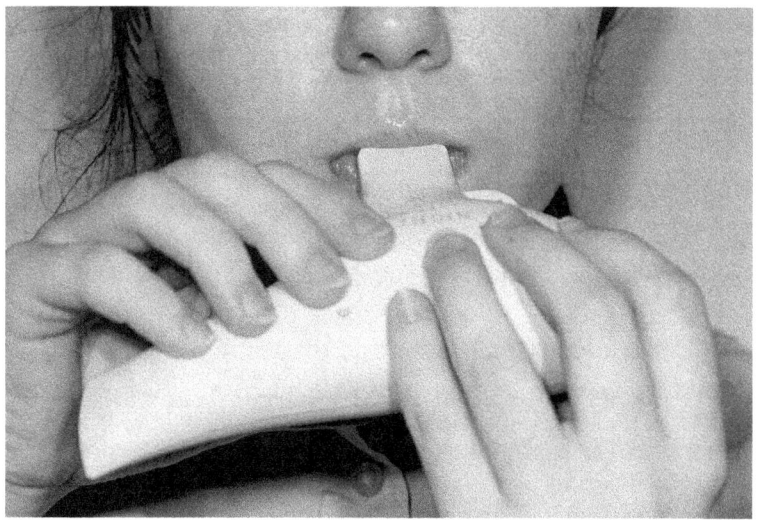

Thankfully, the ocarina is a simple instrument when it comes to initially producing a note. However, a lot of practice and effort can be required to produce a good, consistent sound on this instrument.

If this is your first time hearing an ocarina, you may notice that this instrument has a phenomenally unique and beautiful sound. It keeps the qualities of wind through its gently hollow music.

1. C Solo Note

If you followed the suggested fingering, the note that you just played was a low C! You will learn more about how to read these notes as time goes on.

You may have noticed that this note may not have sounded perfect or perhaps dissonant to your ears. This is okay! As a beginner, it will take time for you to get used to your instrument. You can, if you are interested, spend the time trying to get this note in tune, but do not feel the need to push yourself towards already being 'perfect' on this instrument. It will take time to get used to the feeling of this instrument in your hands and for you to be comfortable immediately producing a quality sound.

Continue playing around with this low C! Notice how your posture affects the quality of the sound or how you can change your breath control. Something so beautiful about music is how small, physical changes can change the artistic quality you produce. So do not be scared to make some noise!

Tuning Your Instrument

Depending on your previous musical experience, you may or may not be aware of the process required to tune your instrument.

A musician is going to tune their instrument for multiple reasons. First off, you want to make sure you are hitting the correct pitches while playing so your music comes across as intended for yourself and your listeners. Secondly, you will want to be in tune because, if you ever were to play with someone else, you want to be playing the pitches in tune so the notes don't sound dissonant (i.e., bad or disagreeable) when heard together. If one person were to play a note in tune while the other did not, it would be noticeable.

When you play your instrument and produce a note, your ocarina is going to make **vibrations** throughout the body of the instrument. By moving through the body of the instrument and out through the whistler of the ocarina, these vibrations become **sound waves**, which is the noise that you hear. Sound waves are measured in **hertz**.

So, when your instrument is tuned correctly, your sound waves will have a consistent hertz reading that will make your vibrations and sounds consistent with other players.

It is possible to determine whether an ocarina is out of tune either by ear or with a tuner, depending on your musical experience or natural inclinations to musical tuning. A poorly tuned ocarina may produce lackluster copies of the songs you are playing. To fix this, you will have to play around with the tuning of your ocarina.

For most instruments, you make tuning adjustments with moveable parts (i.e., the head joint of a flute can be pushed in or pulled out, the tines of a kalimba can be moved up or down, and the saxophone mouthpiece can be pulled out or pushed in). This is not possible with the ocarina. The body of the ocarina cannot be moved or adjusted, so every single part of tuning this instrument must be done in your playing.

Ocarina tuning can be done by adjusting the air that you blow into the mouthpiece of the instrument. As you get more advanced in your playing, you will learn what sounds correct, what does not, and how to fix this. By changing the amount of air used and the speed of your air going into the instrument, you will be able to adjust the frequency of the sound waves your ocarina produces slightly.

Lower notes use less, slower air, while **higher notes** use more, faster air.

Do keep in mind, however, that some instruments can be incredibly low quality or are 'vanity' instruments not intended for serious play. These instruments are often nearly impossible to play in tune. The barrier to entry for these vanity instruments placed on a new player can be incredibly frustrating, and that is why this guide previously emphasized the importance of getting a properly made ocarina.

As you start learning how to play the ocarina, you can attempt to tune your instrument by memorizing the airflow required to produce a steady note. This can be done by listening to a computer-generated sound of your intended pitch until you can match it consistently. You are going to have to play around with this, but it is an incredibly rewarding experience to be able to get the required muscle memory for the ocarina locked in.

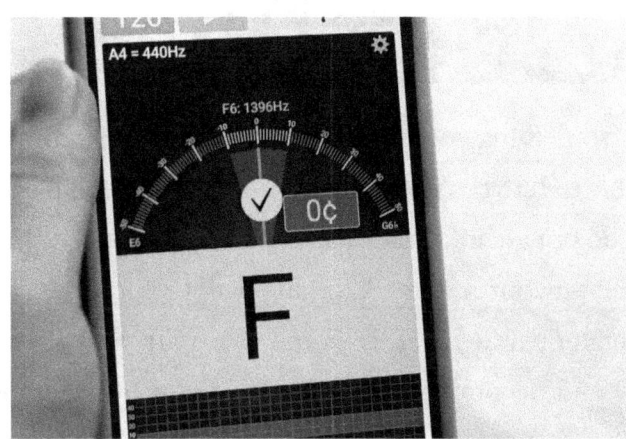

If you are looking for tools to help you tune your instrument, a **tuner** is all you need.

If you have a smartphone, you can find a tuner on the app store. There are many free ones if you do not want to spend money on getting a tuner.

However, there are also physical tuners. Oftentimes, it can be nice to have a physical device at your side while playing. This also encourages you to remain focused on your playing and nothing more.

When you are playing, your tuner will pick up the hertz of the sound waves and tell you what pitch your ocarina is producing, along with how **sharp** or **flat** said pitch is.

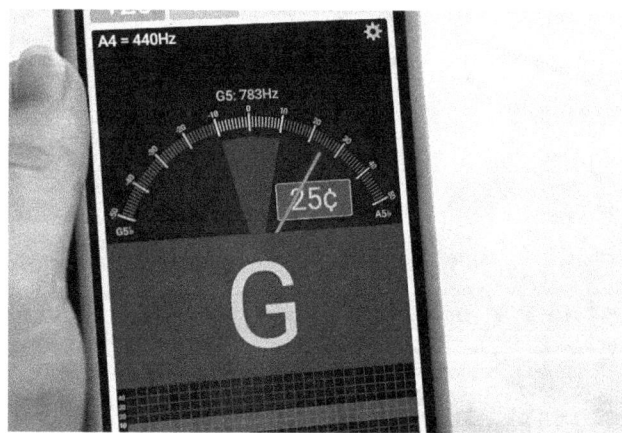

This is something good to know when jumping into the ocarina, as being able to hit your desired note is a fundamental part of music. However, do not get too stressed about being 'perfect' or hitting each note in tune on your first try. Working with the ocarina over time to produce high-quality notes is a massive part of mastering your instrument and becoming a musician. For now, it is a good idea to get a feel for the sound of the tuned notes so that you can healthily recognize when you are playing these notes correctly. Memorize that satisfaction and carry it with you going forward.

Keeping Your Fingers Moving—Learning More Notes

The ocarina requires you to know the correct fingerings so you can produce your required notes. For example, when it came to that low C you just played, you needed to know which finger holes to cover to make that sound.

A massive part of beginner play on the ocarina is about learning these fingerings.

Keeping in mind that this guide is written for the most common type of ocarina—the 12-hole Alto C ocarina—, this is the fingering chart that has been provided. It includes all the essential starting notes but does not cover the full range of your instrument; further fingering charts will be included alongside your intermediate materials.

12-hole Alto C Ocarina – Beginner Fingering Chart

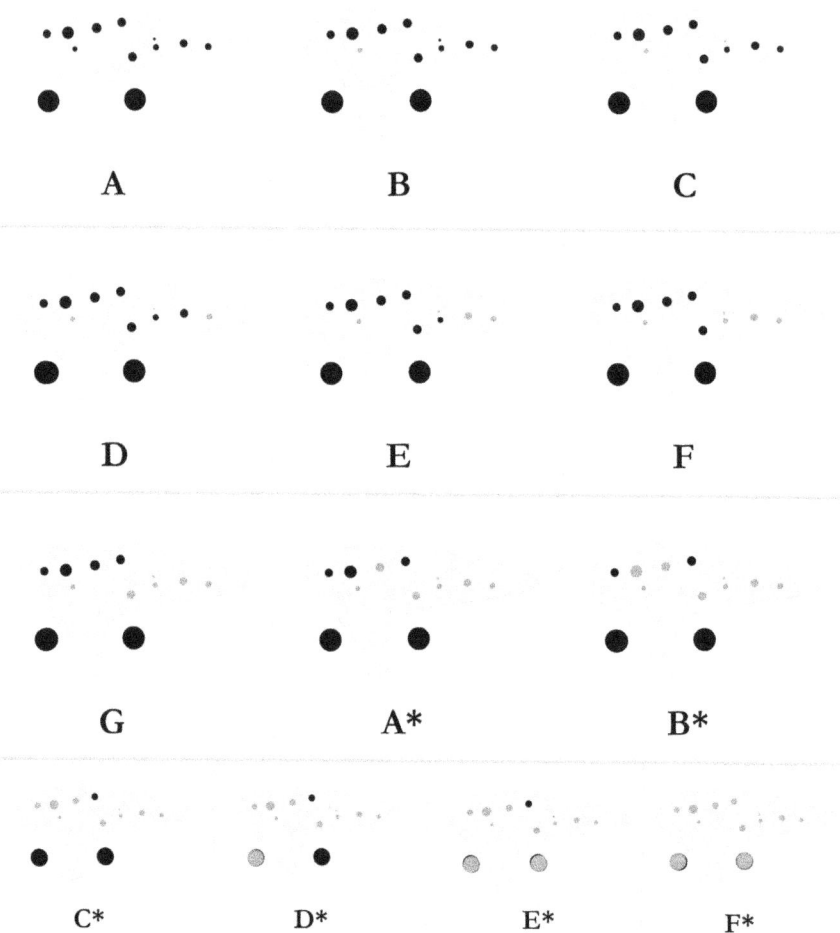

*Stars indicate a higher octave, which means that the note maintains the same pitch but at a higher level. One star means one octave above your middle range.

Most ocarinas—especially ones that have been made for beginners—are going to come with their own fingering charts, but you can reference these when learning the basics and beyond.

If you are having any issues determining the note(s) your ocarina is producing, feel free to grab your tuner. This may be especially difficult if you are unaware of the exact fingerings for your ocarina, but trial and error can be especially helpful if you have an abnormal instrument. By blowing into your instrument and seeing the results on your tuner, you can determine the note you are playing.

The ocarina has a wide musical range, not in terms of tone but rather with the types of melodies available for you to play. This instrument is simultaneously mellow and energetic, meaning that there is a variety of publicly available sheet music adapted for the ocarina. Whether you are playing slow or fast, the ocarina can keep up with you.

Learning how to play multiple notes in succession is an important first lesson in developing your ocarina skills. A fantastic way to begin this process is to play a musical scale.

A musical scale is an organized collection of notes ordered by pitch. Going through and practicing your scales will prove a valuable exercise for your knowledge base, as well as teaching you the required muscle memory for each note fingering in the scale. This will allow you to get used to the layout of your instrument.

Since you may not be immediately aware of the note-to-fingering translation, a visual guide for the note's fingering has been included alongside the notes to the scale.

C Major Scale

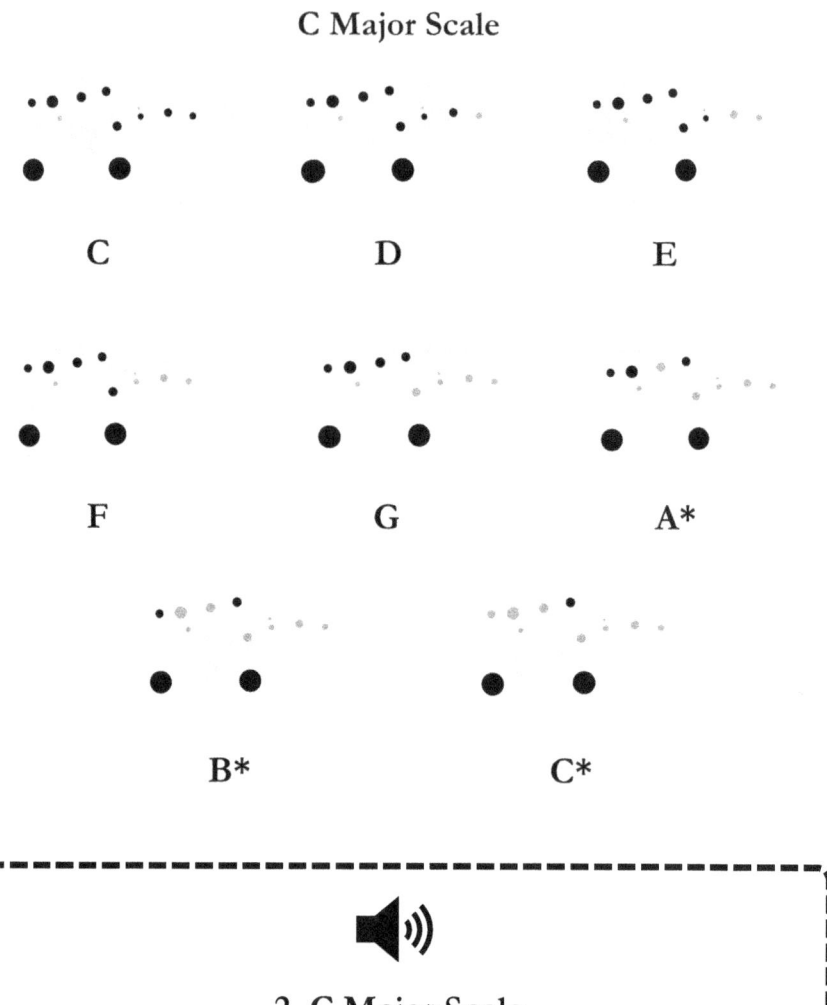

As this guide assumes that most players are still new to playing instruments, sheet music has not been attached for a C major scale. Later steps of the guide, however, will detail how to read sheet music.

When first learning how to play scales, do not be scared to take your time and keep practicing! It will take time for you to master this scale, and that is okay. It is a valuable fundamental that you can build upon before moving into more intermediate or advanced pieces.

Another good beginner exercise is the arpeggio.

The arpeggio is an exercise that breaks apart a musical scale, specifically taking some notes within a chord from the scale and playing them in succession. They can be played in any order; however, they have been organized below for your convenience.

Arpeggios are also extremely helpful as you learn how to play the ocarina. They can help you learn how to move your fingers consistently and smoothly.

Try this exercise:

C Major Arpeggio

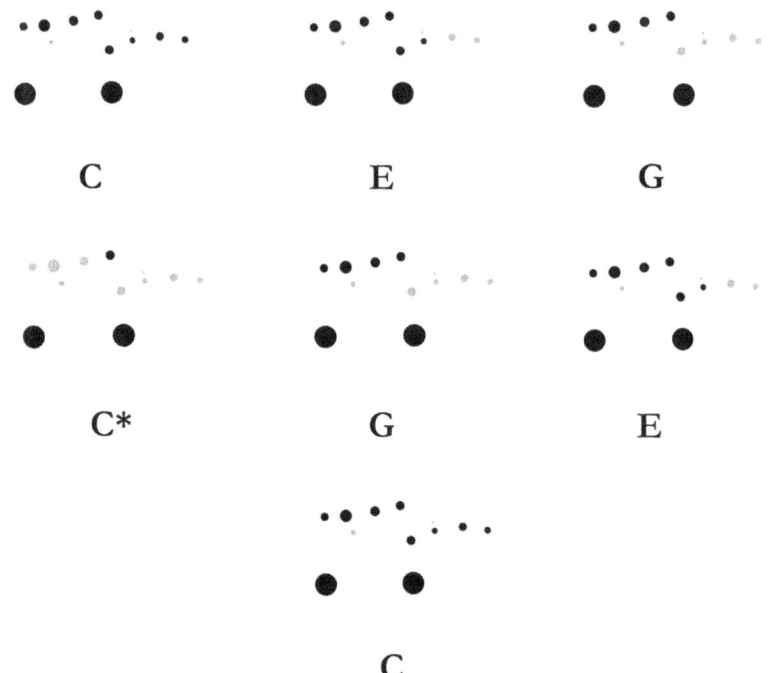

C   E   G

C*   G   E

C

3. C Major Arpeggio

Crafting Melodies

A **melody** refers to a sequence of notes played in a given order with a specified rhythm. A good melody is often easily recognizable, matches the intended tone or vibe of the song, and—when played in a group or band setting—sticks out from other instrument parts.

Melodies in classical music—along with music that considers music theory—are created by considering the pitches in major or minor scales. Previously, you learned how to play the C major scale. These scales can be used to influence the energy and direction of the piece, along with the chords and resolving notes the composer may want to use.

Rhythm is notated in sheet music to show just how the composer or arranger wanted the notes of the piece to be played. Playing a given rhythm too fast or too slow can add or take away from a piece of music! The phrasing of a song has a massive impact on the final product.

To test out your musical phrasing, try playing around with this collection of notes and see if you can find an engaging melody within the short piece below.

Hint: it's a song commonly played at birthday celebrations!

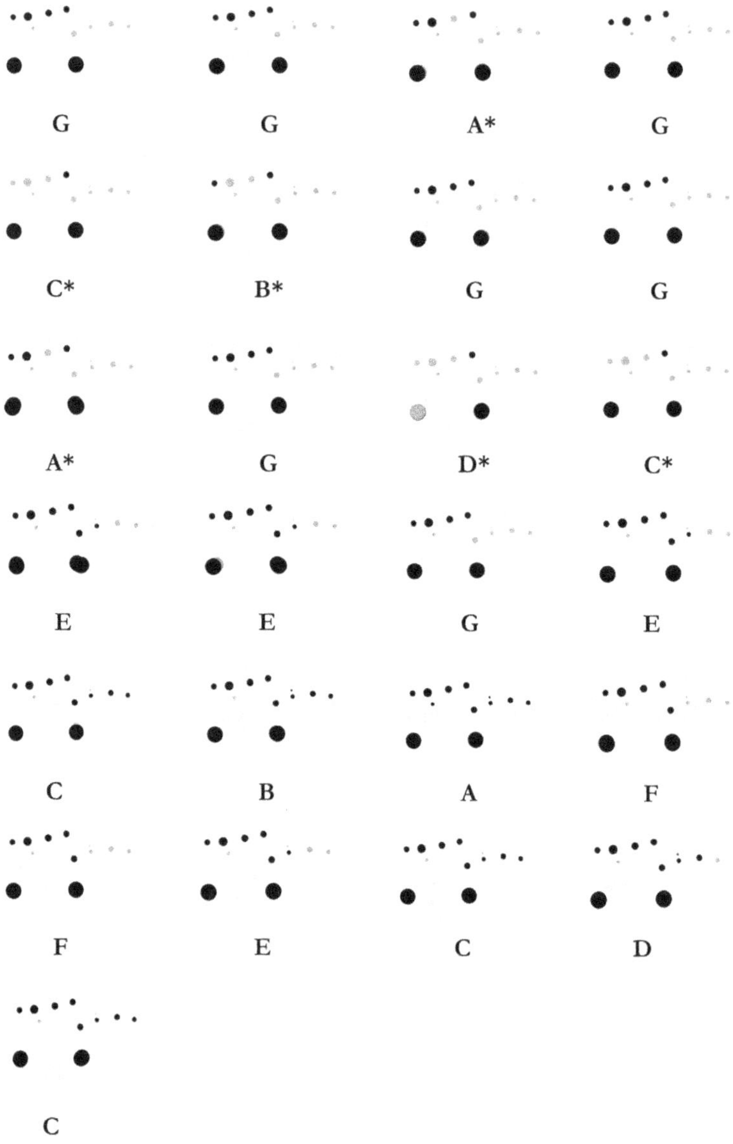

G   G   A*   G

C*   B*   G   G

A*   G   D*   C*

E   E   G   E

C   B   A   F

F   E   C   D

C

4. Happy Birthday

If you struggle with playing melodies in the beginning, don't stress too much about it. It will take time, but eventually, you will be more familiar with your instrument and will be able to play complex melodies. Practice is a necessity, so do not be scared to keep going. One day, after all the time you have spent struggling, you will be able to finish playing a beautiful song. Then, you can look back and see just how far your musical journey has taken you.

Chapter 5

Reading Sheet Music & Music Theory

Explaining the Tablature

The **tablature** is a way of reading sheet music based on how your hands are positioned on the instrument. This is especially helpful when you are learning how to play the ocarina, as it gets you primed to memorize the fingerings for your instrument. This is a valuable skill to develop so that, moving forward, you can read sheet music with ease.

While there is not a lot of ocarina music written out in tablature—meaning you will also learn how to read sheet music—it can be a very helpful learning tool. That is why several ocarina songs have been written out in this guide in the tablature.

While it certainly isn't impossible to jump right into sheet music as a beginner, it adds another barrier to entry that could potentially prevent you from continuing forward in the learning process. By starting in tablature, you can dip your toes into the world of playing the ocarina without first having to learn how to understand the oft-complicated world of reading sheet music.

However, the tablature is most definitely not the ideal way to play the ocarina in the long term. While the tablature for instruments such as the guitar is easy to understand and translate into your hands, this is not always the case for the ocarina. This is because there are so many small finger holes on the ocarina that it is not easy to directly translate a picture into your hands, especially when it comes to more complex music. In the beginning stages of learning, there are many benefits to focusing on your hand placement, though.

As defined previously, the tablature is created around the mental framing of how you place your hands on your instrument. By emphasizing the fingering, you can create a mental link between notes and hand placement.

The ocarina tablature appears as a small illustration of the instrument, with shaded spots over the finger holes you need to cover. This essentially tells you what pitch you should be playing by giving you the directions to do so.

There is no common way for the ocarina tablature to communicate the rhythm of a given musical passage, so this is why the ocarina tablature is incredibly limited. Unless you know the rhythm of a musical work before playing the piece, you are likely not going to be able to play anything as the composer or arranger intended.

Try playing the following. If you do not know the rhythm to Hot Cross Buns, listen along to the audio example and play the notes below accordingly:

Hot Cross Buns

*for ease of use, if the same note is played twice
in a row, the fingering is only showed once

B   A   G   B   A   G

***   ***

B   B   B   B   A   A   A   A

B   A   G

5. Hot Cross Buns

As seen in the example above, some people will combine sheet music with tablature to create a unique musical notation for the ocarina. Because of this, you should learn how to read rhythms in sheet music.

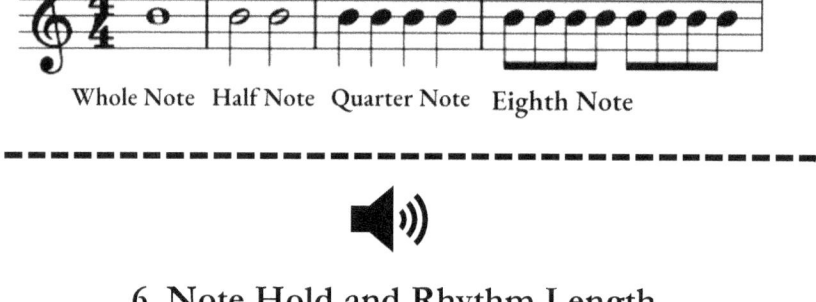

Whole Note   Half Note   Quarter Note   Eighth Note

6. Note Hold and Rhythm Length

The above are basic rhythms you are going to often encounter. Each of the rhythms has a specific duration of time associated with them to communicate how long you should be playing a given pitch.

A measure of music is going to be broken down into **beats**. A beat is determined by the time signature at the start of the measure.

Many of the first songs you will learn how to play will be written in **4/4**. This means that the quarter note is given the beat and that there will be four beats per measure. When playing a measure of 4/4, you can subdivide longer notes into individual beats by counting "1-2-3-4" out in your head. This will help you determine how long to play a given note or rhythm.

For example, the **whole note** is held for 4 beats. This takes up the entire measure or four quarter note's worth of space. For a whole note, you will sustain the note without tonguing or taking a pause throughout, as creating separation within the note may potentially disturb the rhythm.

Furthermore, the **half note** is given half the time of the whole note. This means that the half note is given 2 beats. The **quarter note** is given a single beat, while the **eighth note** gets half a beat.

Subdivision is an important part of the process of reading and playing music. When playing a whole note, for example, you are going to need to break the note down into smaller parts so that you can stay on beat. If you lose track of the beat, you can easily hold a note out for too long or not long enough.

You can subdivide by keeping a constant track of the beat in your head. While playing, you can tap your foot to the beat, for example. Knowing what beat you are on will make sure you play for the accurate amount of time every time.

Subdivision will become especially important the further you break down notes. While you will need to subdivide whole and half notes, mastering the skill of subdivision is even more important for eighth and smaller notes.

You can subdivide for eighth notes by breaking the beat down even further. Instead of going "1-2-3-4", you would say to yourself, "1 and 2 and 3 and 4 and". This will often be notated as 1+2+3+4+.

So long as you keep the beat consistent and don't slow down or speed up, that's all that matters.

If you start learning how to read rhythms with songs that you are already familiar with, it will be easier for you to associate the attached beat values with the look of certain stems and rhythms.

Try reading this piece on tablature. It is a classic that most beginners will play on any instrument!

Ode to Joy

*for ease of use, if the same note is played twice
in a row, the fingering is only showed once

7. Ode to Joy - Tablature

You may have noticed that some rhythms were placed in a different vertical position on the musical staff above (and that the notes' pitches were no longer provided for you!).

The vertical position of a given rhythm on the musical staff indicates what **pitch** you are supposed to be playing. With the help of the tablature, are you able to figure out the pitch of each note you just played? Pitch reading will be covered in detail as you learn more about reading sheet music.

As you start getting better at reading sheet music and the tablature, you will also be able to better understand your instrument. It takes some time to be able to instantly associate your fingering position with a given note, but this is a necessary skill to have.

While you are playing around with the tablature, here is another common lullaby: Twinkle Twinkle Little Star.

Twinkle Twinkle Little Star

*for ease of use, if the same note is played twice
in a row, the fingering is only showed once

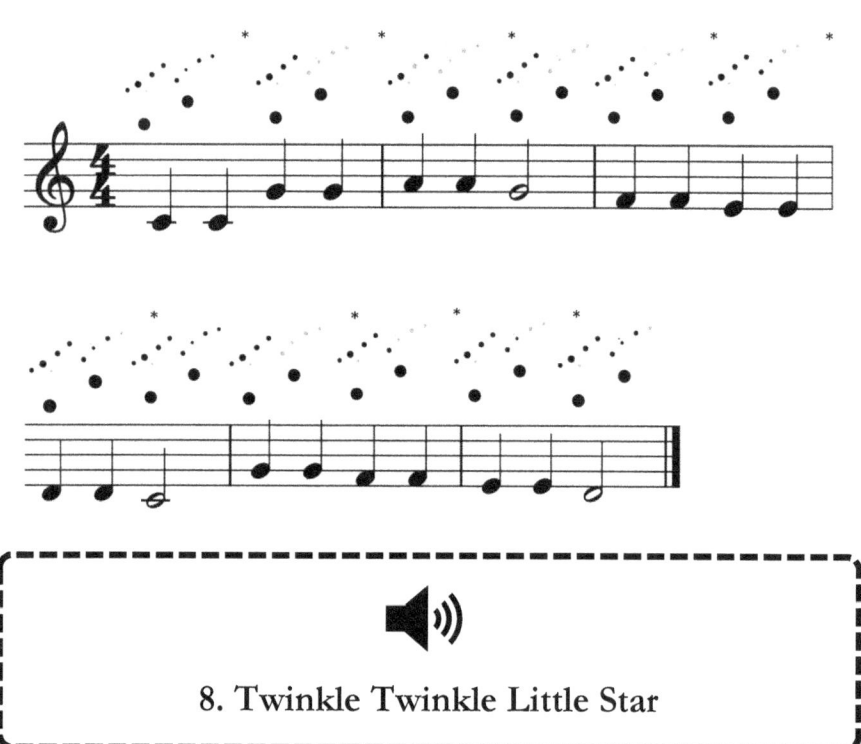

8. Twinkle Twinkle Little Star

The tablature works well for some instruments, but it is certainly not best suited for the ocarina. That is why this guide encourages it only for initial play, as relying heavily on this method of play will likely only hinder you going forward. This isn't to say that you must rush through your application of the tablature. However, it is important to keep in mind that sheet music is going to open significantly more doors for you and allow you to play a wider range of music with less potential confusion and complications. That is why this guide quickly moves into learning another musical skill: to make you a more balanced player overall.

How to Read Sheet Music

Learning how to read sheet music and getting good at it can initially feel as alienating as learning a new language. Thankfully, in this case, it won't take you years to master the reading of sheet music. Since all sheet music uses the same basic structure and bones to convey ideas, once you know how to read some of it, you know how to read all of it, with some research required here or there.

The structural guide for sheet music is called the **staff.** A basic diagram is shown below.

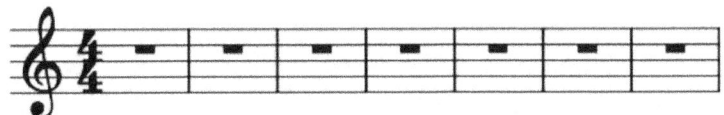

Understanding the staff is essential, as it creates a framework through which all music can be constructed. This formatting can take some time to get used to, so don't stress if it doesn't yet make any sense to you.

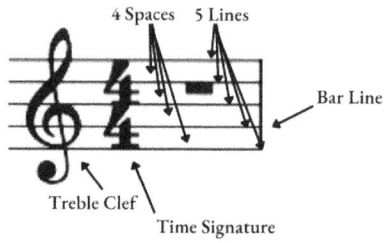

The staff includes **five lines** and **four spaces.** A note will be placed either on one of the lines or in the spaces to indicate which pitch should be played. That note can have any number of rhythms.

Additionally, notes can go above or beneath the staff. When this occurs, additional lines will be added beneath, above, or on the note to indicate its pitch, as well. You will encounter these later in your ocarina playing.

If you are playing a standard 12-hole Alto C ocarina, your music will be written in **treble clef**. The clef, which is positioned at the start of the staff, indicates which range you will be playing in. Treble clef is the most common clef type, but you may also encounter bass clef, which assumes that you are playing on a lower-octave instrument and translates the notes as such. This translation occurs so that you don't have to try and figure out what note is found seven or eight bars beneath the treble clef musical staff.

The **time signature** is found at the start of every piece—and sometimes found throughout the work if the time signature changes for whatever reason—and it indicates what rhythm is going to get the beat and how many beats there are per measure.

The most common time signatures you are going to see will be **4/4** and **3/4**. The first number indicates how many beats there are per measure (in these examples, there are four and three beats per measure, respectfully). The second shows what gets the beat. The four in both time signatures makes it clear that the quarter note gets the beat. So, a measure of **4/4** will have four beats per measure, equaling four quarter notes, two half notes, or one whole note. In contrast, a measure of **3/4** will have three beats per measure, equaling a three-quarter note or one dotted half note. The dotted half note contains three beats, as the dot adds half the original note's length back into the overall playing time. These are rare in beginner music, but you will likely see them the more advanced you become.

Note that when you read the time signature aloud, you would read 4/4 (as an example) as "four, four," as opposed to "four out of four."

Finally, each measure will be capped off with a **bar line**. The time signature dictates the length of a measure, and the bar line enforces that by showing the player where the measure starts and stops. This is helpful when it comes to advanced passages of music that require more subdivision. It also can be helpful when it comes to phrasing your music, as melodies are usually formed around the understanding that they should start and stop at the beginning and end of measures.

While these elements may not seem important yet, they are essential. Think of them as small gears that help your music function. Without the time signature, for example, it would be exponentially more difficult to play your music as the original artist intended. So don't skip over these fundamental lessons, and make sure you understand them well before moving on.

Reading Musical Notes

Learning how to read notes can seem daunting at first, but it is an essential skill. With practice, you will be able to look at music and instantly identify each note and then translate that into what fingering is required on your ocarina. There are also mnemonic devices you can use to remember your notes until you have memorized their location.

As mentioned previously, there are five lines and four spaces on the staff. While all the notes are near each other, the slight differences in their placement make all the difference.

While you are learning the names of the notes, you can use this trick to remember the notes in the 'spaces': **"FACE"** stands for each pitch in ascending order.

F A C E

On the five lines of the staff, there are also notes associated with each placement. These notes are **E, G, B, D, and F**, starting at the very bottom of the staff and going up to the top. Since these notes don't spell out a word, people often use the mnemonic device: **Every Good Boy Deserves Fudge.**

E G B D F

These tips will help you become familiar with the musical staff. A combination of these mnemonic devices, as well as writing down the notes beneath the staff, will help you get used to seeing a location and matching it instantly to a pitch. If you are struggling to memorize the location of the notes initially, use the mnemonic devices and then write down the notes based on what you know from the memorization techniques. Do this until you can identify everything off the top of your head.

There are also notes beneath and above the musical staff. You will not have to play many of these. However, you can determine what notes fall beneath the staff by reversing the order of the notes you learned above; if the staff is ordered as E, F, G, A, B, C, D, E, F, you can observe that the note likely to come before low E would be D, C, B, and A. The notes that would appear above F on the staff would be F, G, A, B, C, D, E, etc. The notes appear in a consistent pattern, so it is possible to use this cycle to read your music if you are ever confused.

Learning how to read sheet music well and instantaneously takes a lot of time and practice. So long as you practice, you will inevitably notice results that will make all the difference. Eventually, you will be able to read sheet music fluently, and that feeling will be so incredibly satisfying, especially since you started from knowing nothing.

Sharps, Flats, and Key Signatures

You have already learned a lot of the basics about sheet music. However, some additional essentials are required if you hope to have a good base-level understanding of sheet music.

One thing you may encounter as you begin to play are **sharps** and **flats.** Traditionally, the ocarina is an instrument that does not play a lot of sharps and flats. However, the more advanced your music is, the more likely you are to come across these.

Sharps and flats are also known as **accidentals**. Essentially, they can either raise or lower the pitch of a note by half a step, as opposed to a whole step.

For example, the difference between the note of C and the note of D is a whole step. In contrast, the difference between the note of Bb and the note of C is only a half step.

In sheet music, **flats** are notated by a little 'b,' meaning that they are a half-step 'down' from the **natural** (meaning neither sharp nor flat) interval.

Sharps are, inversely, indicated by a shape appearing like a number sign or hashtag. These are a half-step higher than their whole-step counterparts.

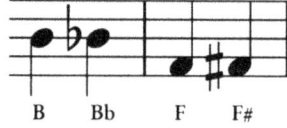

When you are initially learning how to play the ocarina, you will not come across many sharps or flats. This is because the sharps and flats add another wrinkle to your musical equation. Intermediate music will begin to emphasize the full range of your instrument and may require you to play sharps or flats based on the piece you are playing.

Sharps and flats require unique fingerings that are not quite as self-explanatory as their natural counterparts. A comprehensive fingering chart, including sharps, flats, and naturals, is included below. Notes above and beneath the staff have also been included for reference.

12-hole Alto C Ocarina – Chromatic Fingering Chart

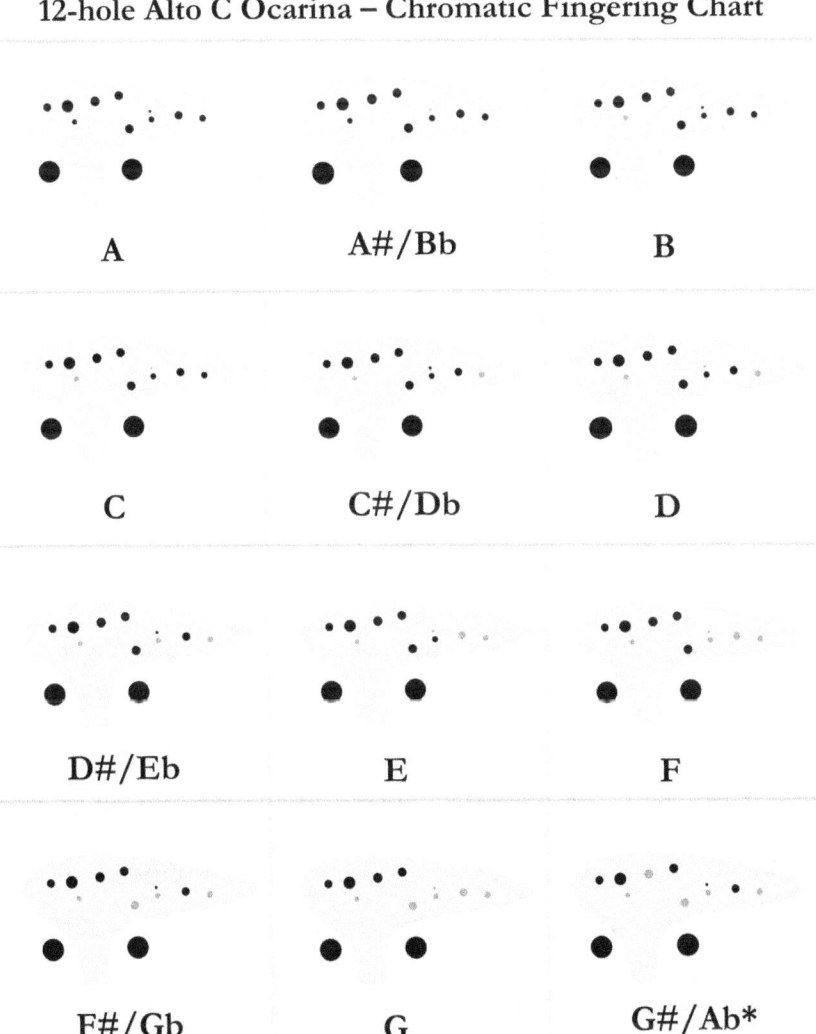

*Stars indicate a higher octave, which means that the note maintains the same pitch but at a higher level. One star means one octave above your middle range.

Chromatic Fingering Chart Pg. 2

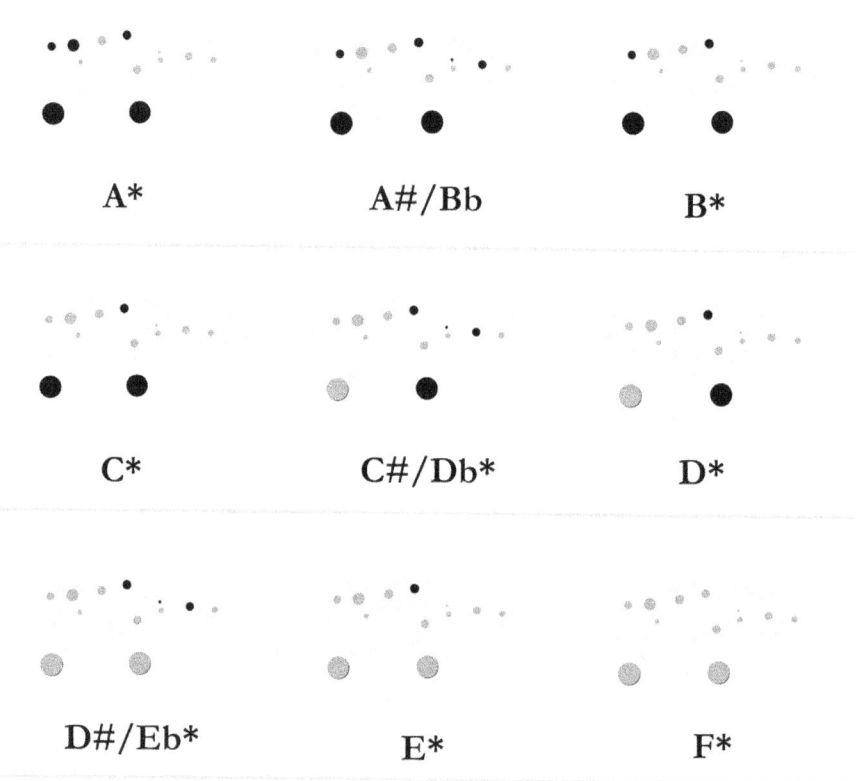

A key signature is going to indicate which natural notes you should be playing as sharps or flats. The key signature is found beside your time signature or the beginning of a new measure after the bar line, where it will indicate what **key** you are playing.

Previously, you have learned about keys. Remember, your ocarina is tuned to the key of C major, meaning that the instrument and fingering method are based on this scale.

There are other keys you can play in, as well, and these keys are denoted by your key signature.

While sharps and flats can be found next to individual notes, as shown above, they are usually found in the key signature, as indicated below.

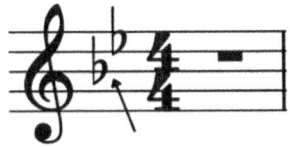

The example key signature is a very common one. If you notice, it has two flats, appearing on the 'B' line and 'E' space. Because this key has a Bb and an Eb, this means that the key of this piece is Bb major.

Most beginner ocarina pieces will not have any key signature indication before the time signature, and this is because the key of C major is one of the best for learning.

Major and **minor scales** can be built around these key signatures. These scales are important as they provide a framework for melodies and harmonies. They can create sounds that are bright, happy, sad, or confusing. Major scales will usually tend to sound 'happier' while minor scales may evoke more sadness.

Major and minor scales are made from a variety of different sharps, flats, or naturals. Below, there is a list of all the major and minor scales. With the above comprehensive fingering guides, you will be able to play through these and notice the differences between all the scales, especially if you are interested in learning the unique nature of these sounds.

Based on the difficulty of the music you are playing, your key signature may vary. Getting used to and quickly being able to read a unique key signature will help you in these instances.

Reading Time Signatures and Rhythms

The **time signature** has been explained previously within this guide. However, given the importance of the time signature—as it proceeds to frame your entire understanding of rhythm and how you should be able to read sheet music, an intermediate definition will be provided.

To understand a time signature, you first should look at the top number to determine the number of beats per measure. Then, look at the bottom number to figure out the type of note that is equal to one beat.

Common 'bottom numbers' include 4 (quarter note), 8 (eighth note), and 2 (half note).

Being super tuned in to the time signature can help you determine the rhythmic framework of the music you are playing, as well as let you play correctly and anticipate the musical beats before they come.

With that recap in mind, we can move into counting rhythms.

Our traditional understanding of music tells us that all songs have a beat. While there have historically always been songs that play around with this idea of being 'free' of a given beat, these are uncommon and are still based on the listener's expectations for what 'music' is.

When playing a song, it's important to find the beat of the music and keep it steady. Maintaining a steady beat is crucial, as this creates a foundation on top of which the rest of your music can happen.

Oftentimes, you may be able to feel the beat naturally. Being able to 'feel' the beat in a song means that you can stick with the flow of your piece naturally without having to do too much counting or additional subdivision.

A great way to get better at feeling the beat is to listen to some of your favorite songs and tap your foot or clap your hands along with the beat of the piece. See how you can naturally fit into the music! Try to guess where musical phrases and measures start and stop.

This is a phenomenal way to better understand the fundamentals of rhythm.

The same rhythms can be found in nearly every type of music, no matter how difficult or what the style is.

These are some of the most common, as have been previously described:

Whole Note Half Note Quarter Note Eighth Note

When new to reading sheet music, it is a good idea to pencil in your rhythms before playing; knowing your time signature will tell you the total number of beats in a measure and will help you ensure you did not make any mistakes in your rhythmic counting.

When describing musical rhythm, each beat is given a number.

In the example below, the quarter note receives the beat, meaning that a quarter note will get one count. And, since it is also in 4/4 time, there will be four beats in a measure.

That means that the rhythm of this piece will be counted out: 1-2-3-4, 1-2-3-4, 1-2-3-4. The speed of the rhythm will typically be noted by the composer, but, in this case, you can go at whatever speed you would like.

A half note gets two counts. It looks like a quarter note but isn't completely colored black.

When playing a half note, you sustain the pitch for 2 beats. For the ocarina, this means you sustain the air in your instrument for a whole two beats without taking a breath until the end of the note.

A whole note is going to receive four counts. A whole note looks like an open circle. It lacks a stem, which is the downward line seen on quarter notes and half notes.

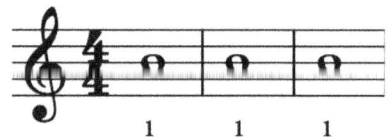

Like the half note, you sustain the air in your ocarina for a whole four beats. If you need to, you can sneak a breath in the middle of a whole note, but know that this may break up the rhythm of the song and sound strange to listeners. It is best only to break the flow of the sound and rhythm by breathing at the end of these whole notes.

Eighth notes are another common rhythm. Eighth notes receive only half a beat. Mastery of the eighth note will allow you to create more complex and quick-moving rhythms.

With an eighth note, you can fit two of them into the length of a one-quarter note.

When counting the rhythm of an eighth note, the first eighth note will get the beat. In this instance, it means that the first eighth note will be counted out with a "1", as has been done previously with all the other notes so far, to indicate the start of each new beat.

The second eighth note is counted with an "and." So, if you were to count a measure of eighth notes out loud, it would sound like, "1-and-2-and-3-and-4-and".

Eighth notes look somewhat like quarter notes but maintain a unique stem. They can be found alone or grouped with another eighth note.

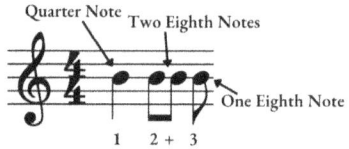

Whole Note = 4 Beats

Half Note = 2 Beats

Quarter Note = 1 Beat

Eighth Note = ½ Beat

These are the most common rhythms in beginner ocarina music. These are fundamental to your understanding of sheet music, so be sure that you are certain in your knowledge of these rhythms before moving on.

More advanced rhythms, while still possible for you to play with a lot of practice, can be saved for when you are a more intermediate player.

Along with rhythms indicating when you should be playing, there are also musical notations telling you when you should not be.

A **rest** indicates silence. You should not play during these instances to maintain the melody and rhythm of the overall piece.

The most common rests are the whole rest, half rest, and quarter rest.

Whole Rest   Half Rests   Quarter Rests

Each of these rests will get the same number of counts or beats as the corresponding note above.

Whole Rest = 4 Beats

Half Rest = 2 Beats

Quarter Rest = 1 Beat

While the **whole rest** and **half rest** may look similar, they are different based on where they lie on the staff. Notice the difference in the picture above and/or below.

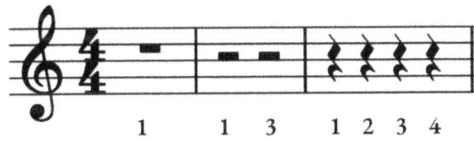

Like earlier, there are also **eighth rests**, which count for half a beat of silence. These are more common in intermediate music, however.

In the beginning, learning rhythms can be one of the most overwhelming parts of playing the ocarina. It can take anyone a long time to learn these complex ideas.

But as you start to play the same pieces over and over, you are going to discover that these rhythms feel familiar and good underneath your fingers.

It's a difficult learning curve to master, but it is worth it.

Chapter 6

Practice Songs

Now that you have learned all about music theory and the essentials for playing, you are ready to apply these ideas into practice.

Music is best learned on the job, so take the knowledge that has been given to you and keep moving forward, challenging yourself, and learning from those challenges.

The Tablature in Practice

This guide has previously provided you with tablature songs. However, as you work towards applying the fundamentals of sheet music to your playing, a combination of tablature and sheet music will be provided for the next few songs. This will help you get used to the fingerings required for the included notes, as well as let you read through sheet music on your own for the first time.

Amazing Grace

9. Amazing Grace

Old MacDonald Had a Farm

🔊))

10. Old MacDonald Had a Farm

Sheet Music in Practice

Now that you have worked through the tablature, it's time to play sheet music!

Since you have not yet been required to identify notes at first glance, don't be scared to take your time with these songs. Use the mnemonic devices that you previously learned, such as FACE and Every Good Boy Deserves Fudge. Penciling the notes in can be incredibly helpful, as can writing out the rhythm for the piece or whatever else you may need. At this point, you are hopefully familiar with the fingering required by the ocarina.

Ode to Joy

11. Ode to Joy - Sheet Music

Auld Lang Syne

12. Auld Lang Syne

Itsy Bitsy Spider

13. Itsy Bitsy Spider

Technique-Building Exercises

Your musical technique is a fancy way of describing your skill or ability to play the ocarina. Technique-building exercises teach you how to play common techniques. For example, one technique-building exercise is the C major scale you learned earlier. Learning this scale means that you can now play these notes at a variety of speeds. It also provides you with the opportunity to get the muscle memory for this arrangement of pitches. Songs written in a given key will likely include **runs**—a quick section of many notes—and these often follow the movement of the **major, minor, or chromatic scales.**

Below is a picture of common scales. Playing these scales before you start every practice session is a great way to memorize them, as well as get yourself warmed up for new pieces.

Scales for Technique Building

Along with major and minor scales, there are also arpeggios. An **arpeggio** breaks apart a chord in a scale and separates the notes so that you are required to play through them in different orders and at varying speeds.

Scales for Technique Building

As you start reading more and more complex music, you are going to notice that some notes go above and beneath the staff, as seen above. Previously, you learned the fingerings for some of these notes. Keep in mind that the reason these pitches aren't centered on the staff is that they are either going to be an octave above or below your middle range.

The pattern of musical notes goes: **E F G A B C D**. This cycle repeats once you reach the beginning or end, so you can use this to reverse-engineer reading these new notes! Additionally, you can use this to work on memorizing the location of all musical notes so you can play them instantly when sightreading a new song. **Sightreading** is when you are playing through a piece of music for the first time without getting the opportunity to put markings in it, noting the rhythms or pitch values. This is a valuable skill to have in a band setting.

Along with the provided arpeggios, you should continue to practice the songs as provided in both tablature and sheet music earlier. You should feel confident in your ability to read these pieces, as these are the jumping-off point for intermediate pieces that are going to require more technique, ability, and music-reading skills to be played well.

Take the time to feel comfortable using these skills before moving on to more intermediate work! Building a strong base is both helpful and necessary to fully master the ocarina.

Chapter 7

Introduction to Intermediate Play

Topics Covered:

- Articulation

- Dynamics

- Tonguing

- New rhythms

Now that you have worked through the basics of this instrument, you are ready for intermediate ocarina techniques.

This chapter will cover musical terms and ideas that you will come across as a newer musician. These ideas will not be related to your ability to play music, but they are required to play music *well*.

You will likely have heard of many of these topics before, but implementing them into your music is another story that involves practice and a good understanding of how your body affects the music created by your ocarina.

In this chapter, you will get more accustomed to advanced musical techniques to truly level up your playing ability.

Articulation

The **articulation** of a piece refers to how you breathe into your ocarina and how you control your tongue while doing so.

How you choose to articulate a piece of music is going to impact the ultimate sound you are producing. Putting more force into the air you breathe into your ocarina will produce a heavier, harder sound than breathing gently into the instrument. Some songs will require proper articulation to be played to their fullest potential.

If the song you are playing requires a distinct articulation, it is going to be marked in the music. If there is no marking given, you may either play with your creative liberty or play 'neutrally'.

One common example of articulated notes includes *no* articulation. This is when you **slur** notes together, also known as a **slurred phrase.**

When you slur a group of notes together, you do not put a break between the notes. You do not breathe in between notes, and you do not tongue. **Tonguing** is when you briefly push your tongue against the roof of your mouth to create a break in the stream of air going into your instrument. This is what you would do when playing a series of normal, non-articulated notes. This does not happen when you slur your notes together, however.

Slurred notes are notated with a line over the top connecting the notes.

One musical notation that may appear like the slur is a **tie.** The tie is a curved line connecting two or more of the same notes in a sequence. A tie indicates an extension of overall note length, as opposed to creating a larger, flowing melody.

The tie is used in music if the composer wants to include a longer rhythm that would otherwise be broken by the bar line.

Other types of articulation also affect the way that you play individual notes, as well.

A **tenuto** is an example of a more intermediate articulation marking. It looks like a small, horizontal line overtop the note you are going to be playing. This marking indicates that you should play the notes smoothly while holding the note for its full length.

Another common articulation is the **staccato**. These will appear as small notes above or beneath the note (based on the individual note's placement on the staff). This is a marking that tells you to play each note shortly and separately.

So, when you play staccatos, you will put more emphasis on the very start of the beat and then soften your air afterward. Be sure not to let your notes 'bleed' into each other as you might for a tenuto, slur, or tie.

There are many types of articulations and variations of holds, but the last one that this guide will cover is the **accent.** These can be identified by the "greater than" symbol above or below a specific note.

An accent is telling you to bring out the sound of a specific note. You can do this by blowing more air into your instrument and creating a louder and more noticeable sound. This, however, may cause your ocarina to be out of tune, which is also not desired.

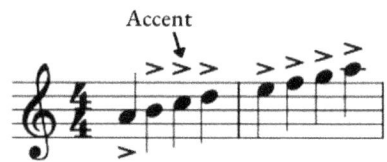

These five articulation styles are going to allow you to start playing more and more music. Not only are these important elements to having good sound quality, but they will also challenge your playing abilities. By adding more texture to how you play, your music will be more fun to play and more engaging to listen to.

Articulation Recap

Slur or Tie = connected notes

Tenuto = long hold, soft attack (-)

Staccato = short hold, quick attack (·)

Accent = emphasized and strong attack (>)

Dynamics

Like articulation, **dynamics** refers to the volume and quality at which you can or should play a section of music. Dynamic markings will be found beneath the staff, and they will typically carry through until the next dynamic marking.

There are many dynamics, and each of them is going to inform your playing of a specific piece.

One problem with the ocarina, however, is that it is very difficult to play dynamically as you would with another instrument, such as the flute or piano. Instead of putting more air into the instrument as you might with the flute or pressing harder on the keys as you would with the piano, this is not possible on the ocarina. If you put more air into the ocarina, it is going to sound out of tune.

One solution to this problem is to play more 'gently' or more 'harshly.' Basically, instead of increasing or decreasing your volume, you use the previous articulations that you have learned to mimic the sensation of changing volume.

Another solution is to just ignore dynamic markings, as you won't be able to play them anyway.

Ultimately, what you do is up to you. However, it is important to know what these markings mean so that way you can play accordingly.

Dynamic markings notated with a **p** will tend to be on the softer side. This **p** stands for **piano**. These can be used for softer lyrical sections, parts of music that aren't the melody, or to create some contrast.

Inversely, dynamic markings with an **f** will be louder. The **f** stands for **forte**. In music, you are going to see louder dynamic markings when you are supposed to play out and be a bit bolder.

However, between, above, and beneath the piano and forte markings are a whole slew of dynamics that will help you create a full roster of sound.

ppp	*pianississimo*	very, very soft
pp	*pianissimo*	very soft
p	*piano*	soft
mp	*mezzo piano*	moderately soft
mf	*mezzo forte*	moderately loud
f	*forte*	loud
ff	*fortissimo*	very loud
fff	*fortississimo*	very, very loud

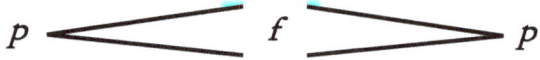

There are a lot of terms used to describe dynamics, so don't be too overwhelmed by them yet. This guide will cover each one in detail.

Mezzo is an Italian phrase for "moderately." This means that mezzo piano (*mp*) and mezzo forte (*mf*) markings should help you bridge the gap between just "loud" and "soft." These two dynamic markings are quite common, and mezzo forte is often considered to be your "normal" or natural playing level. This is what the ocarina plays at all the time.

As previously noted, keep in mind that dynamic markings remain in effect until the next dynamic marking is notated in sheet music.

Along with letter-notated dynamic markings, there are also symbols to indicate a change in sound. This is the case for the **crescendo** and **decrescendo.**

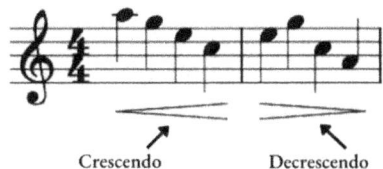

These can also be written out with a line and letters. Keep in mind a decrescendo may also be referred to as a diminuendo.

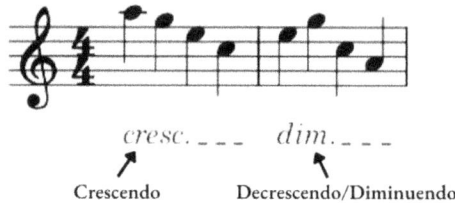

These dynamics will appear beneath the musical staff. When you notice them, you would normally either grow louder or quieter—based on the notation—until you reach the end of said symbol. Depending on the length of your dynamic marking, you would normally have to grow loud quickly or soften as fast as possible. This is not possible on the ocarina, as putting more or less air into the instrument will make it sound out of tune, which is less preferred than missing these dynamic markings.

New Rhythms

With new music, you can expect to find new rhythms.

Here are some common rhythms you may find in your music:

Note Value	Name	Attached Rest Value
	whole	
	half	
	quarter	
	eighth	
	sixteenth	

Remember that all rhythms, no matter how new, scary, or complex they may seem, can be broken down into the beat of the piece you are playing.

Based on your time signature, you are going to know the total number of beats per measure. With that information, you can reverse-engineer the process of reading music by subdividing it down to the smallest possible rhythmic value per measure.

Sixteenth notes are a rhythm that you may discover in intermediate music.

A 4/4 measure of sixteenth notes would be counted out as "1 e + a, 2 e + a, 3 e + a, 4 e + a", with each unique syllable being indicative of one-sixteenth note. Each sixteenth note takes up a quarter of a quarter note.

Exploring Advanced Rhythms in Music

One of the best ways to learn is to apply yourself. So, to test your understanding of the new techniques you have learned throughout this chapter, attempt to play through the following songs, keeping note of the rhythmic values, dynamic markings, and articulations throughout.

Silent Night

14. Silent Night

Greensleeves

15. Greensleeves

Chapter 8

Basic Care and Cleaning of the Instrument

Cleaning Recap

The ocarina is relatively simple to take care of in the long term.

When you are done playing your instrument for the time being, you can clean the outside of the instrument with a polishing or microfiber cloth. You may also run a thin strip of paper through the mouthpiece of the instrument to clean out debris or spit from the body of the instrument.

If you are concerned about the cleanliness of your ocarina beyond this, you may be able to run a lint-free cloth lightly doused in water through the instrument.

Be sure to store your instrument in a safe place where it won't get damaged accidentally!

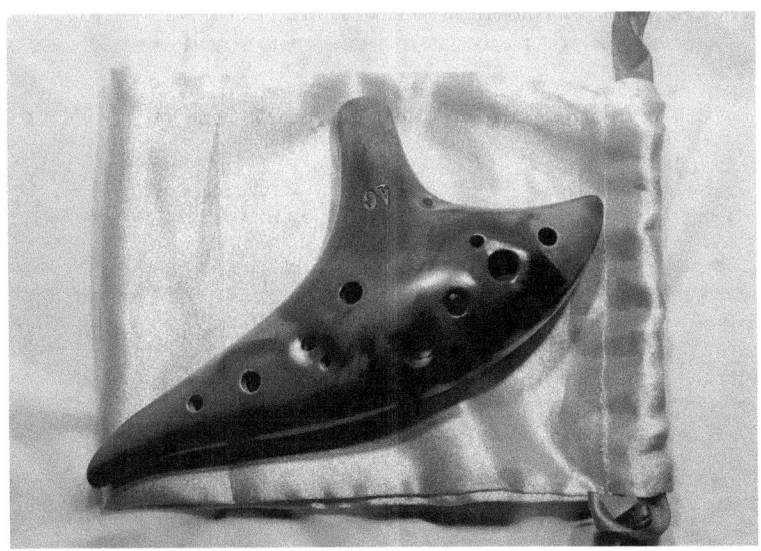

DIY Maintenance Tips

As the ocarina requires very little maintenance, there is not a lot that you need to know to maintain the instrument. Generally, just being sure to keep the instrument clean will prevent all issues.

Again, you can keep your instrument clean with a thin piece of paper and by sliding this paper through the body of the instrument. Some people will also suck and blow out any moisture after playing.

Everything else is common sense. Be sure not to leave the ocarina around on any open surfaces and in some sort of protective box or bag. Additionally, don't play the ocarina with dirty hands, and brush your teeth if you have recently eaten.

Another commonsense measure is to avoid storing the ocarina in damp places for long periods. This can lead to mold, and it is a very difficult process to properly clean the mold from an ocarina. Because of the potential health problems that can be brought on by mold, you want to make sure you are doing everything possible to prevent your instrument from becoming moldy in the first place.

Some people will argue that it is a bad idea to stick anything into the mouthpiece of your ocarina—even a piece of paper or a small needle. This is because it could potentially damage the exit of your ocarina's windway and change the sound quality of your instrument. If this is a concern of yours, you can suck in and blow hard into your instrument after every play session.

Some people will use compressed air instead of doing this.

Ultimately, whatever method is most helpful for you to keep your instrument clean will work. Just always be sure to be gentle on your instrument, no matter the method. Look after it and use common sense to keep it clean. Then, you should not have any issues.

The ocarina generally has very few issues, however, so there are very few maintenance tips required to care for this instrument in the long term.

If you are having a particularly niche issue, you may be able to find the answer to it on the Internet, as there are many people deeply invested in the playing and caring of this instrument. Reach out to any of these sites, people, or forums to see if you can find an answer or solution to your problem.

Chapter 9

Conclusion

Now that you have learned the basics of the ocarina, as well as the intermediate steps, you are no longer a beginner at this instrument! Though there is still so much left for you to learn, if you hope to tackle the challenge of mastering this instrument, you are almost free from the beginner stage!

Recap of Key Learnings

Through reading this guide, you have learned about the ocarina, from its history to its contemporary usage. You have selected the right ocarina for you and learned the required techniques for this instrument.

Additional topics covered have been summarized below.

Key Topics Covered:

- Holding the ocarina

   In this guide, you learned how to properly hold the ocarina so that your grip is natural and not forced. Holding the ocarina should not cause the average person any sort of discomfort.

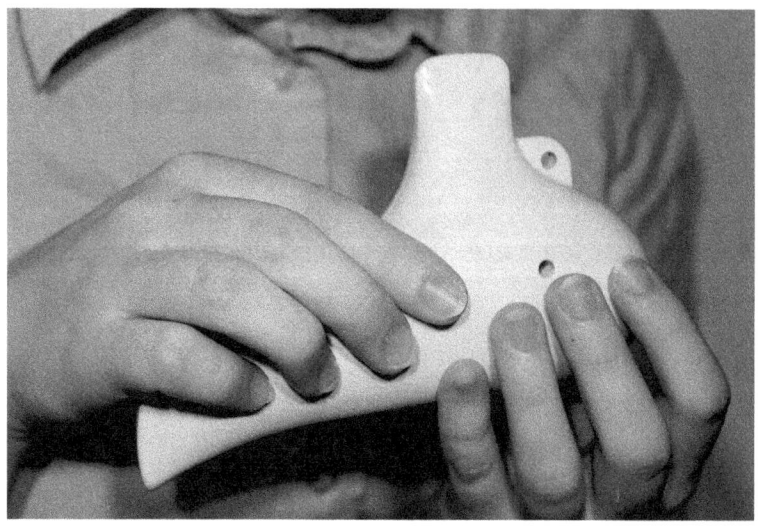

- Playing notes and mastering your range

  Playing notes on the ocarina is also relatively simple: blow into the mouthpiece and match the amount of air you put into the instrument with your fingering. Learning how to master and tune your notes is significantly more difficult, however. Notes must be tuned individually, and with a lot of experience and muscle memory to boot. Tuning your notes on the fly is going to be a massive part of mastering the ocarina.

- Introduction to tablature and sheet music

  This guide covered how to read both tablature and sheet music. While both can be used to play the ocarina, sheet music is important if you hope to experience more professional and masterful play.

- Technique-building exercises

    Technique-building exercises were shared, specifically a variety of scales and arpeggios. Both are incredibly valuable to your long-term playing and can help you get the muscle memory for tuning your notes on the fly!

- Articulation, expression, and dynamic playing

    One of the more recent sections of this guide covered how to articulate and express yourself on the ocarina. This will prove more and more important with harder music that requires specific playing techniques to convey to listeners the melody and the beauty of the song.

Next Steps in Your Ocarina Journey

This guide has offered you the resources to move from complete beginner to intermediate player. Now, you may be wondering where to go from here.

Truthfully, this is only a question you can answer. What about the ocarina calls to you? What do you want to explore? Narrow in on that thing and continue to explore it! Create music and watch it flourish, or spend hours practicing your scales until you can play them effortlessly.

Generally, however, some good steps forward may include learning how to tune all your notes, making sure you can play every note on your ocarina, and getting into more advanced sheet music!

Just don't forget to keep playing and learning. Get out in the world and make beautiful music! Learn from others and embrace the amazing scale of musical possibilities around you.

No matter what, don't ever look back!

Appendix

Resources for Ocarina Players

Tuner Resources

At this point, you have likely already used a tuner for your ocarina. If you don't like the one you have, however, consider trying another option. The tuner is an important tool for any musician to have, so having one that is compatible with you matters! This is especially true with the ocarina, as you will likely have to spend a lot of time repeatedly playing the same note to ensure you have memorized the correct tuning.

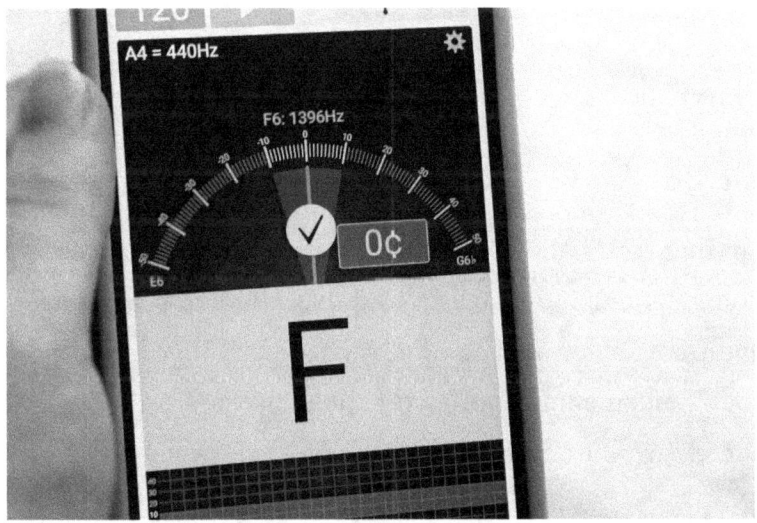

If you are looking for a nice, physical tuner, you can find one at any music store. Many tuners are also available online or on your phone, but they will not have the same physicality and may prove distracting.

If you already have a tuner but don't have a metronome, consider getting another app or device that allows you to have access to a metronome. A **metronome** will allow you to properly keep in time with your music, as it will sound out the beat for you at a consistent pace.

Don't feel the need to go out of your way to get an expensive tuner or metronome. There are plenty of tuner apps out there for free. Try them out in your app store!

Tuner Apps:

- TE Tuner & Metronome

- insTuner

- Chromatic Tuner

Music Books

Getting your hands on a music book will allow you to discover a whole new range of music. Now that you know the basics, you can jump into intermediate or advanced play. If you want to work on your fundamentals more, you could also focus on beginner or advanced beginner music.

Try looking up **popular ocarina songbooks** on the Internet. If you can, purchase the books that interest you the most (particularly by taking a peep at the songs included in these books).

If it interests you, take the time to support small musicians and talented ocarina songwriters.

If you are looking for free or cheap alternatives, there are many options online for free sheet music on the Internet. These can often be played or downloaded without any charge. Keep in mind that learning how to play the ocarina this way is not always as balanced as a compiled ocarina playbook might be.

Continuing to play with music is valuable, so keep pushing yourself! This is the best way to improve.

Websites, Internet Resources, and Ocarina Communities

There are a lot of beneficial techniques that you can learn from other people, so don't be afraid to start looking for ocarina-specific spaces and communities.

Here are a few popular ocarina or music-sharing sites:

- https://theocarinanetwork.com/

- https://pureocarinas.com/

- https://www.facebook.com/groups/284155633176204/

- https://musescore.com/

These will serve you with a variety of different resources that you can use to grow as you move forward on your own ocarina and musical journey.

Unlock Your Musical Potential:
Get 30% Off the Next Step in Your
Instrumental Journey

As a token of appreciation for your dedication, we're excited to offer you an exclusive 30% discount on your next product when you sign up below with your email address.

Visit the link below:
https://bit.ly/40NikR2

OR

Use the QR Code:

Unlocking your musical potential is easier with ongoing guidance and support. Join our community of passionate musicians to elevate your skills and stay updated with the latest tips and tricks.

By signing up, you'll also receive our periodic newsletter with additional insights and resources to enhance your musical journey.

Your privacy is important to us. We won't spam you, and you can unsubscribe anytime.

Don't miss out on this opportunity to continue your musical journey with this special discount. Sign up now, and let's embark on this musical adventure together! 🎼

www.ingramcontent.com/pod-product-compliance
Lightning Source LLC
Chambersburg PA
CBHW070438130626
46553CB00006B/2239